Robert Xavier Rodrígu

PIÑATA

for Orchestra

(full score)

ED 4048

First Printing: October 1998

ISBN 0-7935-8548-1

G. SCHIRMER, Inc.

DISTRIBUTED BY

HAL•LEONARD®
CORPORATION

7777 W. BLUEMOUND RD. P.O. BOX 13819 MILWAUKEE, WI 53213

PROGRAM NOTE

A short, festive crowd-pleaser, *Piñata* blends Mexican folk music, samba rhythms, contemporary symphonic techniques and American jazz. The score includes quotations of two actual Mexican *piñata* songs, *Hora y fuego* and *En las noches de posadas*, which are traditionally sung at fiestas such as birthdays or at Christmas time. After a bustling introduction, the music graphically depicts the swaying *piñata,* a brightly decorated clay pot filled with candy and suspended on a string (in this case, two solo violins). As the excitement builds, there is a series of mighty orchestral whacks at the *piñata*, which eventually breaks open in a triumphant coda. The work may be presented in concert form or as a ballet. Jointly commissioned by the El Paso Symphony and the Dallas Symphony, *Piñata* is regularly performed on subscription, youth and family concerts across the United States.

Piñata was first performed by the El Paso Symphony, conducted by the composer, on March 22 1991; and by the Dallas Symphony, conducted by James Rives Jones, in October 1991.

INSTRUMENTATION

Piccolo
2 Flutes
2 Clarinets in B♭
2 Bassoons
Alto Saxophone in E♭

4 Horns in F
3 Trumpets in C
3 Trombones
Tuba

Timpani

Percussion (3 players):
Glockenspiel, Crotales, Marimba, Vibraphone, Chimes, Glass Wind Chimes, Triangle, Tambourine, Castanets, Claves, Maracas, Suspended Cymbals, Cymbals, Timbales, Congas, Bass Drum

Piano
Harp

Strings

duration: ca. 5 minutes

Performance material is available on rental.

PIÑATA

Robert Xavier Rodríguez

2

poco rit. Andante cantabile ♩ = 92

4

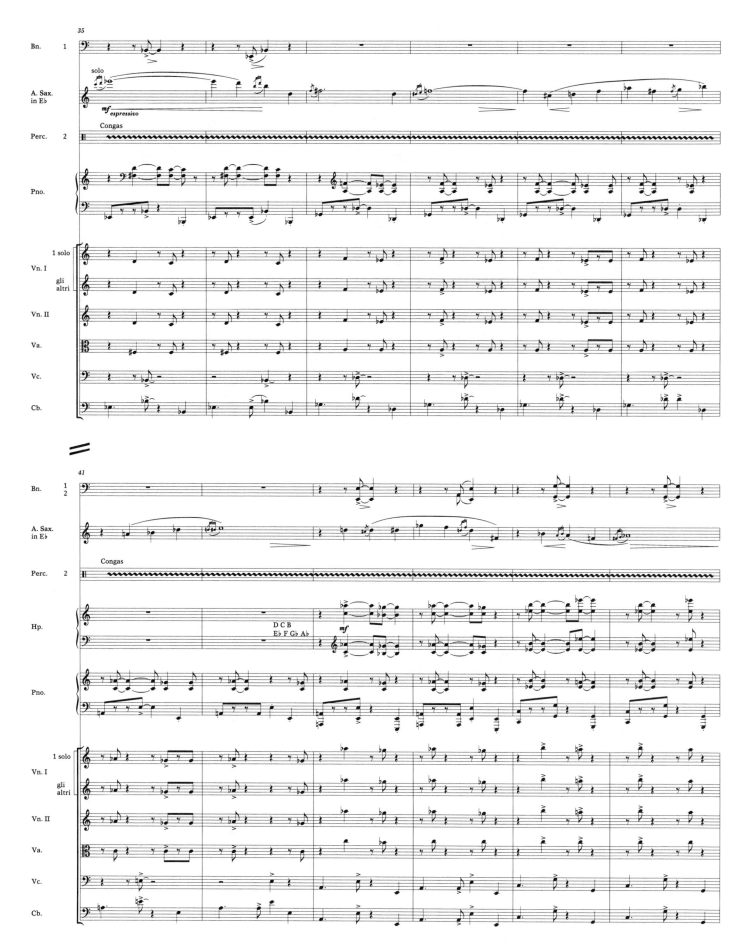

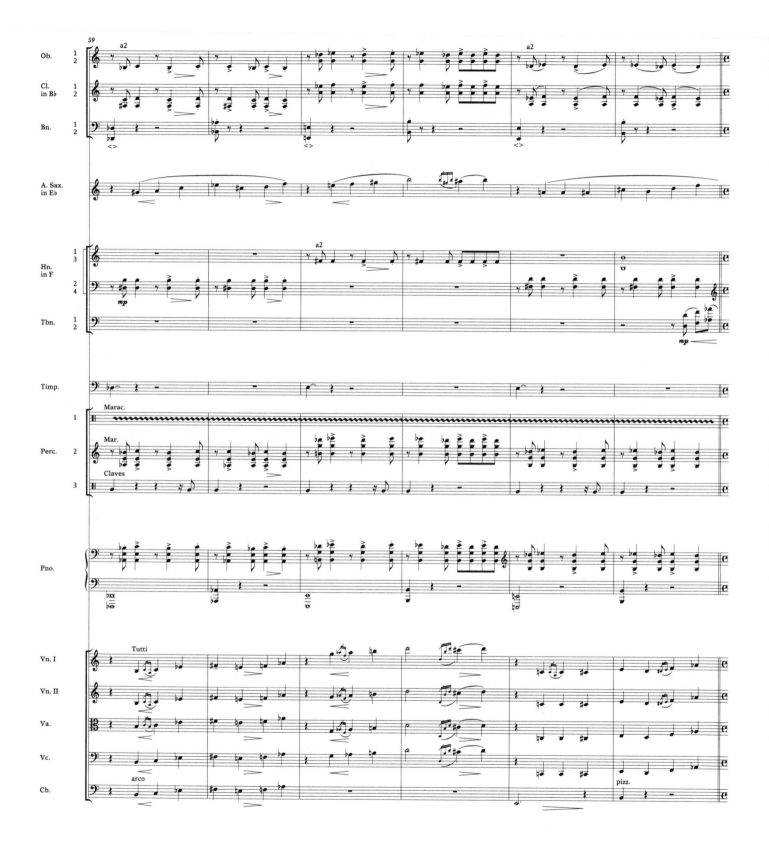

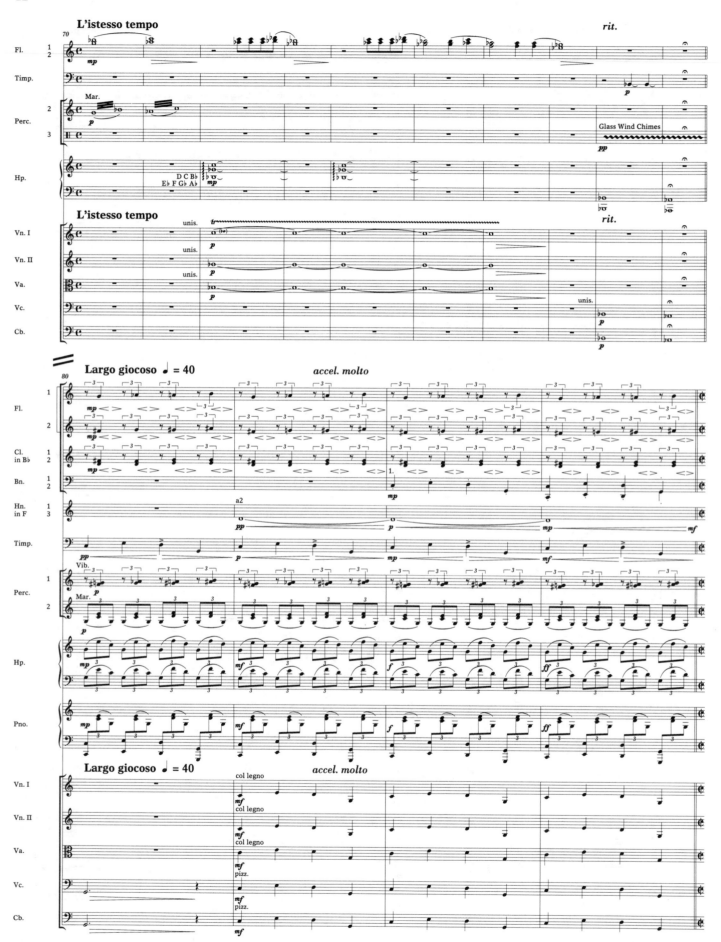

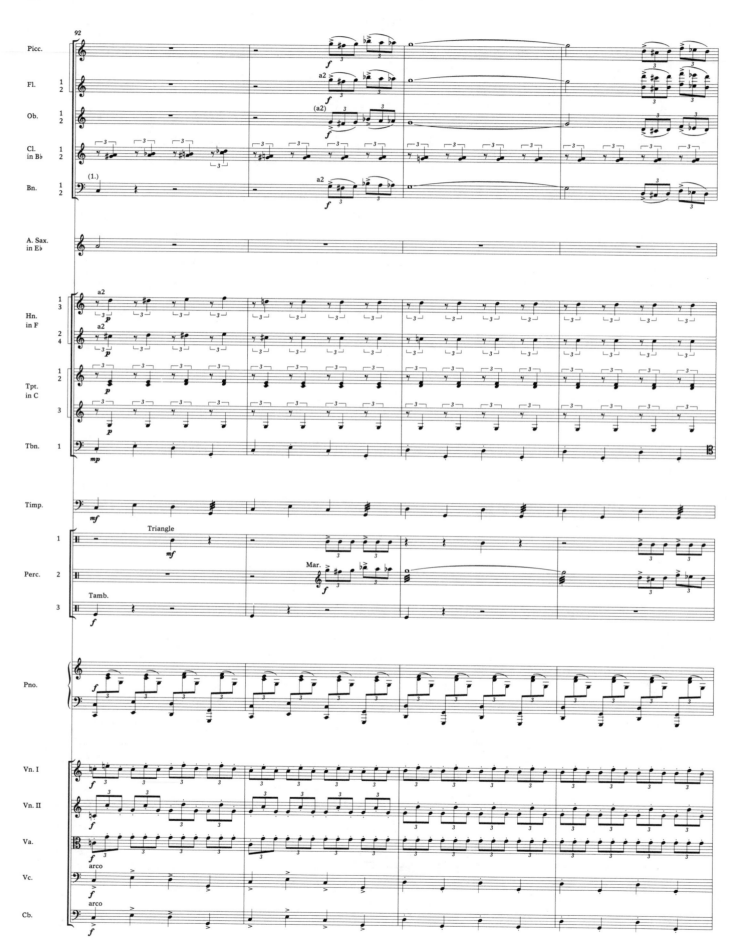

16

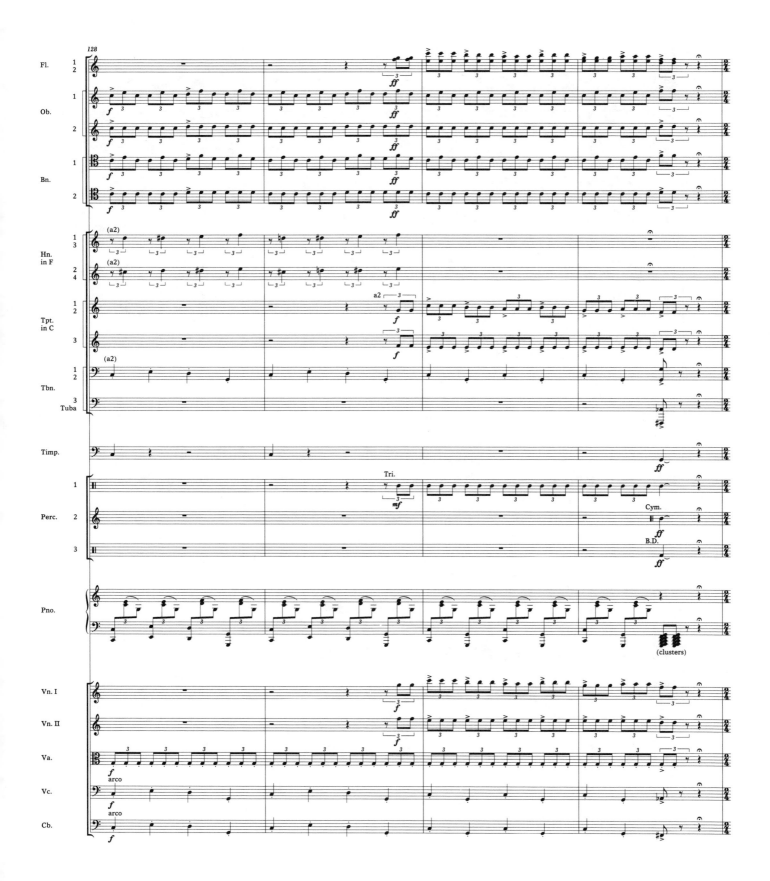

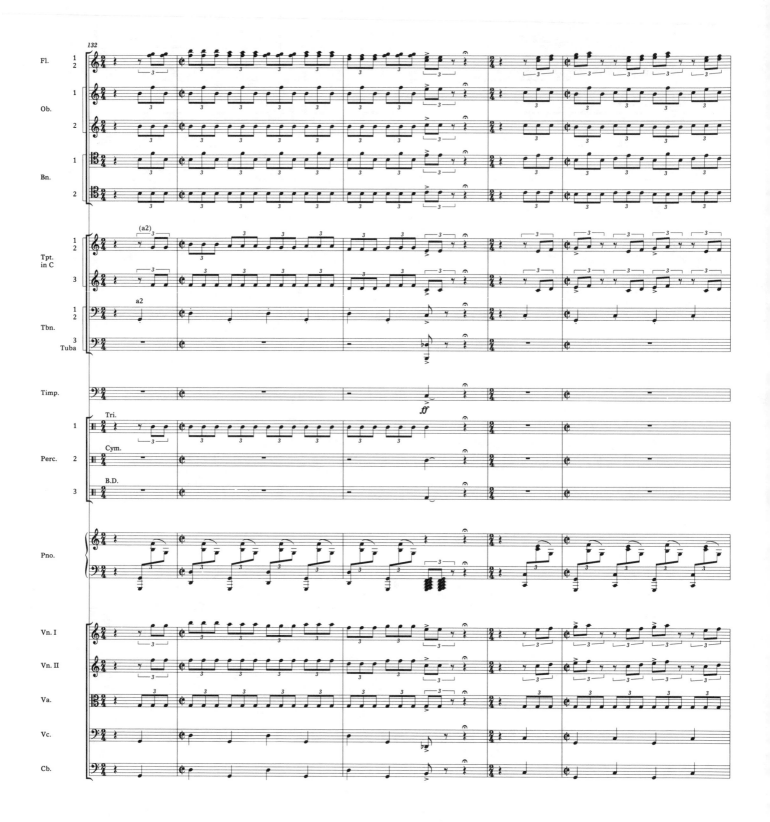

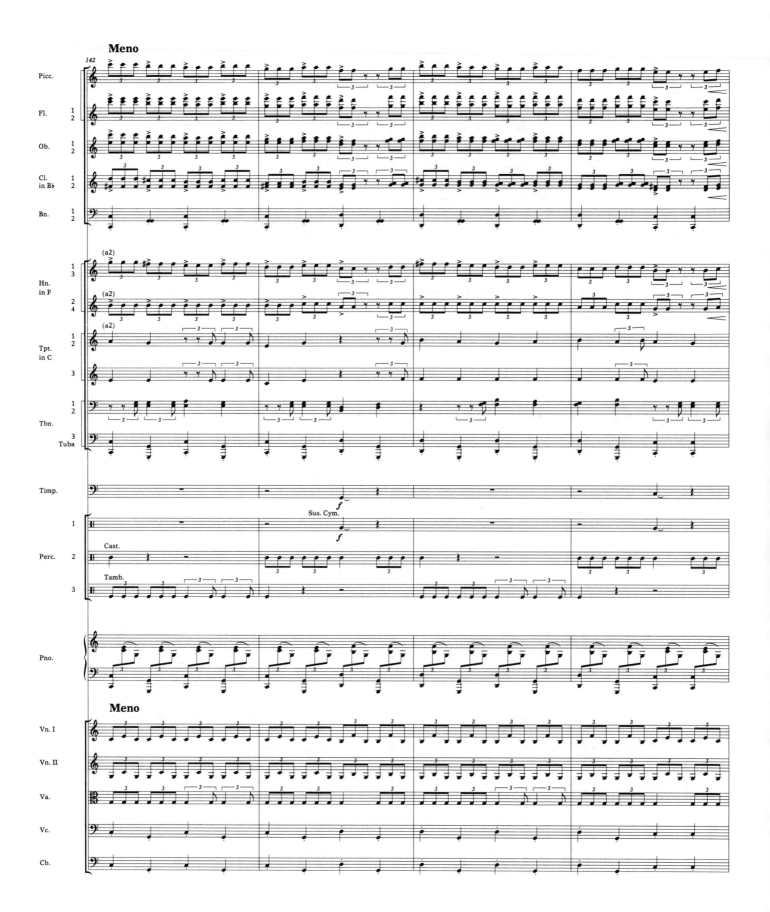